THE 12 PROPHETS OF ALEIJADINHO

THE 12
PROPHETS OF
ALEIJADINHO

PHOTOGRAPHS BY HANS MANN

TEXT BY GRACIELA MANN

80985

UNIVERSITY OF TEXAS PRESS   •   AUSTIN AND LONDON

Library of Congress Catalog Card No. 66–15700
Copyright © 1967 by Hans Mann

Typesetting by Service Typographers, Inc., Indianapolis, Indiana
Printing by Meriden Gravure Company, Meriden, Connecticut
Binding by Universal Bookbindery, Inc., San Antonio, Texas

CONTENTS

ILLUSTRATIONS

THE 12 PROPHETS OF ALEIJADINHO

INTRODUCTION

A fundamental distinction must be made between Spanish and Portuguese South America as regards the conditions and development of colonization. To their surprise, the Spaniards met with empires of long standing and a high level of civilization, and these they had to overcome, not merely by the force of arms that brought the Indian low, but also by a process of adaptation that might harmonize the traits of character, and the political, social, and cultural framework of two worlds in conflict. As a result, in the course of time the termined racial trends of the conquered reappeared, together with the renascence of their deep-rooted artistic traditions, and succeeded often enough, as it were, in indianizing the European.

Very different was the picture that confronted the Portuguese: a land of dense forests, soil that had never been tilled, and a population of naked savages. This is perhaps why Spanish colonial architecture differs so widely from Portuguese, particularly in the churches that were built to accompany the spread of Christianity over the continent.

Around 1700 in colonial Brazil came a discovery to give a new and vigorous turn to the country's evolution. The region now occupied by the state of Minas Gerais, with its vales of purple-red loam hidden in the folds of the mountains, was invaded by a bold, hardy race of men: the *bandeirantes*. Taking their name from the *bandeira* or flag under which they fought their way inland against the hardships and the hostility of the unknown, these large, semimilitary bands of pioneers were seeking the more tangible forms of wealth. At first they came back only with nothing but slaves. In doing this, however, they blazed the first trails into the back country; and indeed there were gold and diamonds to be found in those silent wastes. The sands of the Rio das Velhas, which for centuries had tranquilly kept their secret, were loaded with gold to arouse in the seekers a crazed lust for the precious metal. The colony was still poor, depending exclusively on farming, and the discovery of gold produced hectic disorganization. The towns were emptied, the plantations were abandoned, and the military barracks were deserted. Greed sparkled in the eyes of the travellers as they trekked wearily in from the most out-of-the-way places. Masses of slaves were set to work panning the gravels, and the groups of straggling, hastily constructed dwellings soon acquired cohesion and importance, growing into the towns such as Villa Rica, Mariana, Sabará, São João del Rei, Congonhas do Campo—the gold towns.

Villa Rica grew more lustily and aggressively than the others. It was there that the governor from Portugal took up residence and there that the royal foundry cast the gold into bullion, reserving for the crown the fifth part of all that was found and any diamonds weighing more than twenty-four carats. Striking haphazard up hill and down, the little cobbled streets hastened to keep pace with the rapid spread of the population whose new houses were being built from day to day. Nor was God forgotten in this orgy of Mammon. Stonecutters were at work and churches began to rise. Soon, from one hill to the next, their white towers were greeting one another with a merry peal of bells. Each religious order made a point of having a temple of its own. Luxury and ostentation knew no bounds. Only the richest ornamentation was good enough, and sculptors came from distant cities to carve the images of saints, decorate the places of worship, and set up fountains in the public squares. This—although, or perhaps because, the medley of adventurers that surged into the new-born towns thrilled only to the lure of gold, living recklessly, chaotically, miners and slaves alike.

The heady environment can be felt in the architecture of the times.

The Baroque style was introduced into Brazil by the Jesuit missionaries. It had arisen in Europe toward the end of the sixteenth century, culminating in the splendor of religious architecture in the seventeenth, and declining in the eighteenth. In the hands of the Jesuits, who particularly favored this style, it was developed as an incentive to worship, and the results came to be known as Jesuit Baroque. Intended to "delight the eye by richness and variety of design," it created an atmosphere of sumptuous adornment that made a deep impression on the faithful.

This atmosphere was well suited to Brazil. The physical landscape and the exuberant temperament of the inhabitants required a mode of expression as effusive as the Baroque. Nature would seem to have vied with man in the attainment of beauty. The luxuriant tropical scenery was as much a challenge to him as a stimulus; sensuously insatiate, the artist in him demanded more and felt the urge to erect a fitting complement to the magnificence around him. Forms suggested new forms, and excess was piled on excess. Thus the interior of the churches, in a polychromatic profusion of ornament, radiated a gaiety that was the expression of a transparently ingenuous religious feeling.

Suddenly the gold fever was quenched. The marvellous nuggets no longer gleamed in the river beds and a fortune could no longer be sifted from the sands. Little by little the miners withdrew. Indifferent and disillusioned, they abandoned the towns that had sprung up in the assurance of success. The rhythm of life slackened; silence and the quiet of repose invaded the streets and mantled the old walls. Not far from there, civilization had set a new course and was surging ahead, but in Minas Gerais the past remained entombed and but one name emerges from the silence, that of Antônio Francisco Lisboa, religious sculptor and master carver, whom the people affectionately dubbed Aleijadinho, the Little Cripple.

Graciela and Hans Mann

Congonhas do Campos

THE SCULPTOR OF MINAS

The life of Aleijadinho is obscured by a maze of legend through which it is difficult to trace an exact course, in spite of the numerous books that have been written on the subject. The wide range and uneven quality of his work have opened up a field of conjecture, not only as regards the true authorship of some of it where no definitive supporting data have been preserved, but also as to how he learned his trade. Thus, the facts of his life have been revealed at great effort, with the hammer and chisel of perseverance and criticism carving out the details from the uncertain bedrock of anecdote and tradition, tales told years after his death by persons, often of little education, who remembered having seen or known him.

Manuel Francisco Lisboa, who is supposed to have been Aleijadinho's father, was one of the many who set out from Portugal for the fabulous lands of Minas Gerais at a time when the output of gold was rising to a peak, and he arrived in Villa Rica with nothing but the authorization to work as a carpenter and the ambition to share in the wonderful adventure that everyone was talking about. Among the miners and the slaves, in the surge of colonial expansion where craftsmen were at a premium, he had no difficulty in finding employment. Gradually, as the demand for his services increased, he rose to the position of master builder and sometimes helped with the plans of the churches that he erected.

In 1738, when he was living with a Negress in one of the outlying suburbs of Villa Rica, a son was born to him out of wedlock. This was Aleijadinho, but nothing much is known of the boy's early years until the name Antônio Francisco Lisboa is recorded as that of a twenty-eight–year–old craftsman, working on his own. It would seem that he did not live very long with his mother, but there is no doubt that she handed down to him the gift of her race, the plastic instinct, which inspired and strengthened him in the pursuit of a career that is never easy even at the best of times. The little mulatto was born in and of Brazil, and in him, as in his mother country, the seed of talent took root and grew untended and unobserved.

While he was still a child, his father married, giving him a home where he grew up with his stepbrothers, but it is impossible to judge what influence this may have had on his material upbringing or artistic leanings. The rapid expansion of Villa Rica had already attracted artists from other towns; they and the local craftsmen, however, could not be said to have formed an environment conducive to the progressive, conscious development of Art as such; nor was there anyone to detect or interpret the wavering signs of a vocation in a little colored boy, far less urge him toward a suitable education. He must, therefore, have wandered at will about the building sites where his father was at work, attracted irresistibly to bench and scaffolding, playing at chipping stone and paring timber with, in his clumsy fingers, the very tools that were later to bring him fame and suffering. In the meantime, one way or another, he managed to learn to read and write.

As a very young lad, he must have begun his apprenticeship in his father's workshop and that of his uncle, Antônio Francisco Pombal, later being hired as a journeyman by the master craftsmen engaged in church decorating. Any contact that he may have had with the artists who came to work at Villa Rica can have been merely occasional and superficial. He could only study what they had done, only learn by practical experience. At the same time, living in close touch with the religious communities and perhaps inspired by his own religious fervor, he began working as a church decorator, and in the course of his long career—forty-five years—he never departed from sacred sub-

14

Igreja do Carmo in Ouro Preto

Altar lateral in Igreja do Carmo in Ouro Preto

jects. This contact with the religious orders was a dominating factor in his artistic development, exerting an indirect influence on his cultural background and providing him with a source of inspiration for his work. It was his knowledge of the Scriptures, with the prints and woodcuts which illustrated the Bible, that enabled him to design his woodwork and statues of the Saints, carve his pulpits, and accurately reproduce, for instance, the figure of the Lamb.

He is described, so far as such descriptions are to be trusted, as a cheerful fellow in his youth and early manhood, full of the zest for life and love. He seems to have divided his time with an equal exuberance between work and play, faithfully fulfilling his engagements at Villa Rica and the nearby towns, while leading a joyful, carefree existence, until the appearance of the first signs of the malady with which he was to be afflicted. From then on leprosy or some hereditary venereal disease gradually deformed his limbs and he suffered intense pain, eventually losing several of his fingers and toes, until at last he was reduced to hobbling along on his knees. Realizing that people had begun to look at him with fear and loathing, and nourishing a growing self-hatred in his own breast, he took to working behind a tarpaulin, starting in the early hours of the morning and not going home before late at night. With this radical change in his way of living, his character warped and he sank into an egocentric depression that effectively set him apart from his fellow men.

He owned three slaves, Maurício, Januário, and Agostinho, and they were the only human beings he allowed near him. He had taught them the rudiments of his trade and they gave him whatever help he needed. Maurício generally accompanied his master, fitting the tools to his crippled hands and adjusting the leather kneepads that enabled him to shuffle painfully about and climb the high stepladders he had to use. Januário led the mule that carried him when he ventured farther afield, or when he travelled from one town to another.

He was thirty-nine when he was struck down. For the long, weary years until his death, Aleijadinho went through constant physical and spiritual torture that undoubtedly told on his artistic temperament.

São Francisco de Assis, the church dedicated to Saint Francis of Assisi in Villa Rica, marks the start of his artistic career. Several times in the course of his lifetime, he worked at its adornment leaving the imprint of his personal style on the façade, the flanking arcades, and the interior, as may be seen in the rich retables, the carvings of the chancel, the various groups of saints, and the stone panels that embellish the pulpits. This was the first time he used soapstone, a soft, bluish variety of steatite which is found all over the region and which eventually became his favorite material.

This church is certainly one of his most complete ornamental works. Although in general design it follows the Baroque lines adopted by the local craftsmen of his day, every particular bears the stamp of his own inspiration. The effect he obtained with the ornamental façade so impressed the other religious brotherhoods that he was continually being asked to design something of the kind for their churches. Thus the soapstone façade is now a recurrent feature of ecclesiastical architecture from end to end of Minas; and sometimes it seems to conflict sharply with the rest of the building.

Igreja do São Francisco in Ouro Preto

Igreja do São Francisco in Ouro Preto

Igreja do São Francisco in Ouro Preto

Fountain in the sacristy, São Francisco in Ouro Preto

Chorus, Igreja do Carmo in Sabará

Pulpit, Igreja do Carmo in Sabará

*Saint George
Museu da Inconfidênc
in Ouro Preto*

Unidentified figures, Museu da Inconfidência in Ouro Preto

Street in Congonhas do Campo

CONGONHAS DO CAMPO
Site of Aleijadinho's Masterpiece

Reposing tranquilly in the hills as though swept up by the gold rush like one of the mining townships and stranded there when the high tide of adventure ebbed, Congonhas do Campo is well chosen for Aleijadinho's most appealing achievement: a quiet spot hidden from the curious and the profane behind a curtain of time-worn ridges. There his lonely spirit at last found the peace in which to create, in contrast to the restful scenery, the dramatic figures that tormented his imagination.

For thirty years he had been at work on the churches of Minas Gerais. Now at fifty-eight, exhausted and wracked by the disease that was eroding flesh and bone, he received yet another summons, this time to execute an important project for the Sanctuary of Bom Jesus de Matosinhos, on which he was to labor for nine more years. The commission involved a series of life-sized scenes of the Crucifixion together with twelve statues of the Prophets to adorn the parvis.

To start with, he engaged a large number of helpers to rough out the figures from the massive blocks of stone so as to relieve him of the heavy preliminary routine work. An organized team of stone cutters, carpenters, and wood carvers were on hand to carry out his orders; and subsequent studies indicate that much of the work suffered directly from the failure of these assistants to follow his instructions. At this stage it is impossible to tell with any degree of accuracy how far this is true.

Aleijadinho divided the Crucifixion into six scenes, each corresponding to one of the stations of the Cross, with a retinue of supporting figures and secondary actors in the tragedy vividly represented and carved life-size in wood. Roman soldiers with ferocious expressions prance about grotesquely and contrast with the stiff, jointless bodies of the other characters and with the figure of Christ, which is always treated with greater care and reverence. Some critics have asserted that Aleijadinho himself worked only on the six figures of Christ, that of Mary Magdalene, and those of some of the apostles. Looking upon the achievement as a whole as an example of popular art, we find it to have dramatic quality on a naive, fusty level.

It is possible that these scenes, arranged in stone chapels built in the garden leading to the sanctuary, arouse in the simple folk that visit them as intense a religious feeling as that which inspired their creator.

Bom Jesus de Matosinhos in Congonhas do Campo (seen from a hill behind the church)

FIGURES OF CALVARY

Saint James sleeping

Unidentified figure

Servant during the Holy Supper

Roman soldier, with Mary and child

Unidentified figure

Roman soldier

Roman soldiers

Saint Peter

Judas   Chris

Bom Jesus de Matosinhos in Congonhas do Campo

THE STORY OF THE SANCTUARY
OF BOM JESUS

The Sanctuary has its own story, which begins with a miracle that is said to have befallen a certain Portuguese settler, Feliciano Mendes, who had journeyed to Minas in the elusive hope of making a fortune. After a time, he fell seriously ill and made up his mind to spend his meager savings on a passage back to his mother country, there to end his days in a convent. His prayers, however, were so fervent that the Lord gave him back his health. Overjoyed at so miraculous a cure, Feliciano set aside his plans and vowed he would devote his life to serving God as a hermit. On the top of the hill dominating Congonhas he raised a humble cross, with a niche at its foot for the image of Jesus. Then, clad in a habit of rough blue cloth with his hermit's box slung from his neck, he trudged untiringly through the countryside gathering alms in the little villages. Soon he had enough to transform the niche into an oratory and he begged the ecclesiastical authorities to grant him permission to convert it into a chapel and celebrate Mass there. News of the miracle spread abroad and people came from far and near to venerate the image and pray for grace. Each pilgrim helped to enrich the chapel with what he could afford; the poor would often give all they possessed, while the rich donated lands and livestock, so that year after year the hermit's dream came nearer to fulfillment. By the time he was dead and forgotten the church he had dreamed of stood in place of the cross he had planted so long ago.

The building itself had been completed when Aleijadinho was called to Congonhas. All that was missing was the façade and the statues of the Prophets to stand at the angles of the walls surrounding the forecourt and the double staircase leading to it.

The erection of the last of these statues signified the culmination of Aleijadinho's greatest achievement. All that he had accomplished in the course of his career was ennobled and overshadowed by these impressive figures with their strong lines, carved at how great a cost by agonizing blows of the chisel and mallet secured to his mutilated fingers. When he was sixty or a few years before, while he was working on the statues of the Crucifixion tableaux, he lost his favorite assistant with the death of his slave Maurício. It must have taxed his strength to the utmost to complete the undertaking. Not only did he labor with his own crippled hand, but he had to guide and supervise the company of men engaged in preparing the blocks for the master craftsman to finish. Careful analysis tends to the conclusion that even in the finishing he did not work unaided. In some of the statues, a marked difference can be seen in the treatment of the upper and lower parts of the body, while special pains seem to have been taken with the head and features. It is possible that in certain cases Aleijadinho completely sculpted only the latter, merely putting the finishing touches on the rest of the body, the folds of the raiment and the ornamentation. As in his earlier work, the lack of anatomical proportion is striking and the bodies, often deformed and disjointed, contrast violently with the heads. Nevertheless, viewed as a joint undertaking, the completed project remains a unique plastic ensemble, in close harmony with the building and its surroundings.

When his work at Congonhas was over, Aleijadinho returned to Villa Rica, where he still accepted an occasional commission. In his declining years he agreed to collaborate with one of his disciples, Justino Ferreira de Andrade. Moving his belongings to a house owned by one of the religious orders and adjoining their church, he lived there with Justino. Once again, however, he was fated to be disillusioned, for when he was almost blind and disease had made appalling inroads,

Bom Jesus de Matosinhos

undermining the last vestiges of his health, his ungrateful disciple left the cripple with no one to attend to his wants while he went off to spend Christmas with his own family. The old man had fathered a son when he was past middle age, and now in blank despair he was obliged to struggle to his daughter-in-law's house. There he resigned himself to await the solace of death, but his agony was to be dragged out for two more years. Unable to move from the bare boards on which he was laid, he grumbled incessantly that people owed him money but refused to pay. When at long last he died he was seventy-six years of age.

The pilgrim, on his way up to the Sanctuary of Congonhas, at the

The atrium of Bom Jesus de Matosinhos (Note in the background the construc-tions housing the Stations of Calvary)

top of the hill, passes through the garden where the stations of the Cross are so crudely and touchingly immortalized. After a reverent pause at each, he climbs on by a rough-paved path with grass sprouting between the stones until he comes to the cobbled square surrounding the church. The church itself is built on a higher level so that it must be reached by twin flights of steps, ascending for some seven feet. At the edge of the square, he will be arrested by the imposing sight of the Prophets, confronting each other in grave, wordless colloquy, or, with arms and faces raised to Heaven, outlined against the sky in strange attitudes, with the squat, pinnacled façade of the church in the background. At eventide, the bells ring out cheerfully, calling the faithful. One can sense the soul of the artist, alive in every

one of the statues. His body, unchained by physical agony and spiritual anguish, has dissolved with his earthly existence, even from the memory of men, but his work remains for present and future generations to contemplate.

Graciela Mann

WHEN THE STATUES SPEAK

Gazing over the valley where the Maranhão flows far below, scanning the rolling uplands green-carpeted with the wild holly of Minas, following the lazy meanders of the railway where an occasional train pants up the grade scarce troubling the peace of the ancient mines that no longer echo to the ring of pick and the scrape of shovel—for those who have ears to hear, the Prophets speak.

There—where had his hand lost its cunning?—Antônio Francisco fashioned them in perfect harmony with the parvis, the sanctuary, and the sweeping panorama of Nature, and there—magnificent, terrible, grave, and tender—they talk of worldly matters that, in the language of Holy Writ, acquire an inner, symbolic meaning.

The Baroque beards, caught in the wind that sweeps over the uplands, curl and uncoil like vengeful serpents; shaven, the features of others reveal the strange nobility of wisdom. And the Twelve, robust despite the frailty of the soapstone from which they were carved and the stealthy blows of the devout who covet a holy fragment—the Twelve, in solemn assembly, ponder the state of man's affairs, lament the increasing iniquity of the godless, reprove, and utter many a dire warning.

"A live coal, taken by a seraphim from the altar of the Lord, hath seared my lips," proclaims Isaiah at the foot of the steps.

And Jeremiah, stricken with woe, cannot hold his peace: "My heart maketh a noise within me; I weep, for Judah hath been laid waste and Jerusalem overthrown . . ."

Thus does the complaint of Jeremiah wail through centuries, nor cease even though Israel reassemble the scattered tribes, for there is but one Jerusalem, the Heavenly City, where corruption shall not enter, nor the people and the city be broken by the Lord of Hosts as one breaketh a potter's vessel.

Changeless through the ages, the Prophets are fully as significant today as when they were carved. At any epoch, in any historical situation, the lesson is there to be heeded.

"I show unto Judah the drying up of the vine and the languishing of the fig tree, the rotting of the seed under the clods, and the earth laid waste by the palmer worm and the locust, the cankerworm and the caterpillar," says Joel, the son of Penthuel.

And Habakkuk raises up his left arm to inveigh against the tyrant and the dissolute: "Babylon I accuse! Woe to the Chaldeans, that bitter and hasty nation . . ."

Enthralled in an apocalyptic vision, Ezekiel describes "the whirlwind and the fire enfolding itself, and the four living creatures that came out of the midst thereof, the dreadful wheels within wheels and the throne of sapphire."

Hosea tells of God's judgment on spiritual whoredom, and how the Lord in the sweetness of His mercy, would have the Prophet take unto him an adulteress that she might bear children, and eventually the children of Judah and of Israel shall be gathered together, sons of the living God.

But Nahum, the pessimist, does not believe in the reconversion of outworn values. "Woe to the bloody city! All Nineveh shall be destroyed, for there is no healing of thy bruise, O king of Assyria."

Daniel and Jonah, however, testify that there is hope even for them that be cast into the den of lions (and many such are waiting in disguise to break the bones of the wicked ere ever they come at the bottom of the den); hope for them that disobey the word of the Lord, take ship and flee from Him, only to be cast forth into the tempestuous sea like Jonah and remain for three days in the belly of a great fish.

This is the tenor of the conversation at the fantastic meeting of the Prophets on the windy heights of Minas. Where, indeed, would such a meeting be held if not in the land of Minas, itself a paradox and so deeply imbued with mysticism that the uncouth lust for diamonds, gold, and colored crystals is transmuted to create a wealth of sacred ornamentation, pulpits for the men of God, and pews for the faithful? Though the people of Minas be isolated amid the rock masses of iron ore, they remain in philosophical intercommunication with the world at large, absorbed like none others in studying the ills that beset mankind, in a desire to comprehend and allay them. Life on the mountain pastures brings wisdom and a love for the simple virtues, for kindness, charity, and above all for freedom. Deeply opposed to tyranny, the people of Minas carry the feeling of what is good and just, into a kind of organized frenzy, explosive and contagious, as may be seen in their liberal revolutions.

The Prophets are essentially of Minas Gerais—they are Mineiros: Mineiros in the pathetic, introspective attitudes that Aleijadinho, himself a Mineiro, has given them; Mineiros in their wide comprehension of the world with all its evils, wars, crimes, miseries, and ambitions; Mineiros in their practical common sense and mistrust of soothing cure-alls; in their pessimism; in the inner glow of their mysticism; Mineiros, yes, as much now as a century and a half ago, taciturn, moody, Messianic, and melancholy.

Carlos Drummond de Andrade

THE PROPHETS

ISAIAH

Cum Sera:
phim Domi:
num Celebra:
ssent, a Seraph
uno advola
est Labris for:
cipepuina
meis.
JSAIÆ cap

JEREMIAH

BARUCH

EZEKIEL

DANIEL

HOSEA

JOEL

AMOS

OBADIAH

JONAH

NAHUM

HABAKKUK

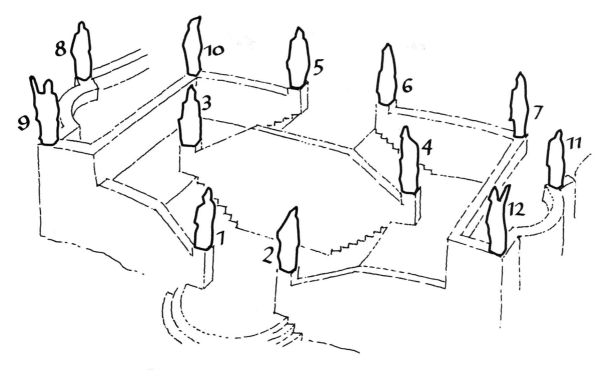

Diagram of the atrium, Bom Jesus de Matosinhos

1. *Isaiah*	5. *Daniel*	9. *Obadiah*
2. *Jeremiah*	6. *Hosea*	10. *Jonah*
3. *Baruch*	7. *Joel*	11. *Nahum*
4. *Ezekiel*	8. *Amos*	12. *Habakkuk*

NOTE

Two of the statues of the Prophets seem to be wrongly placed. A glance at the diagram will show that the artist intended the chronological order of the Bible to be followed. This is broken by the figures of Joel and Jonas (numbers 7 and 10, respectively); the error is confirmed by the position of the body and the direction of the gaze which, in each case, is out of harmony with the arrangement of the other figures in the composition. Artistic and chronological symmetry would be restored merely by interchanging these two statues.

Hans Mann

SELECTED BIBLIOGRAPHY

Azevedo, Fernando de. *A cultura brasileira.* São Paulo: Edições Melhoramentos, 1943.

Carvalho, Feu de. *O Aleijadinho.* Beló Horizonte: Edições Historicas, 1934.

Engracia, P. e. Julio. *Relação cronólogica do santuário e irmandade do Senhor Bom Jesus de Congonhas do Campo no estado de Minas Gerais.* São Paulo: Escolas Profissionais Salesianas, 1908.

Filho, José Mariano. *Antônio Francisco Lisboa.* Rio de Janeiro: Artes Gráficas C. Mendes Junior, 1945.

—. *Estudos de arte brasileira: Antônio Francisco Lisboa.* Rio de Janeiro: Artes Gráficas C. Mendes Junior, 1924.

Freitas, Newton. *El Aleijadinho: Antonio Francisco Lisboa.* Buenos Aires: Editorial Nova, 1944.

Freudenfeld, R. A. *Mestre Antônio Francisco o Aleijadinho.* São Paulo: Inteligência Edições Culturais, n.d.

Kelly, Celso. *Tres gênios rebeldes.* Rio de Janeiro: Serviço de Documentação do Ministerio da Educação e Cultura, 1953.

Pedrosa, Heitor. *O Aleijadinho.* São Paulo: São Paulo Editôra Limitada, 1940.

Penalva, Gastão. *O Aleijadinho de Vila Rica.* Rio de Janeiro: Renascença Editora, 1933.

Zweig, Stefan. *Brasil pais do futuro.* Rio de Janeiro: Editôra Guanabara, 1941.